CHINA

AND

POTTERY

MARKS

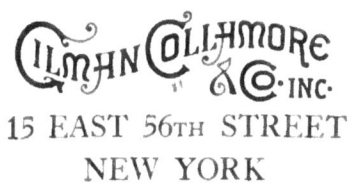

15 EAST 56TH STREET
NEW YORK

Traditions
and Old China

Traditions
and Old China

FROM early days when the ancients showed their appreciation of fine pottery and old glassware by burying "these most esteemed possessions" with the dead, fine china has been synonymous with culture and breeding. With our ancestors for generations we share the tradition that, just as first editions give prestige to one's book shelves, old china or the finest work of the modern kilns express readily that good taste and discrimination that is characteristic of our old families.

A wealth of association and historic data is to be acquired from the study of the "fabrique marks" and periods of the master craftsmen. If in America there was a general tendency toward acquiring, even a smattering, of this knowledge, there would be less of these drawing-room atrocities which Arthur Hayden in his "Chats on English Earthenware" points out, "To have a modern set of vases adorning a Georgian cabinet is like putting new wine in old bottles."

For the convenience of the seasoned collector, as well

as the beginner, in this book is a representative list of better known marks by which china can be identified. While it is not possible to include a complete list, particularly those of extremely rare specimens, those compiled have particular reference to the marks of English china which is greatly in demand by collectors. These will suffice to enable the reader to identify pieces whenever encountered.

The signatures or mark which the master craftsmen in earth or clay signed their products, just as a painter signs his work, were often specially designed devices of various kinds, often a combination of initials and dates. Each "fabrique mark" stands for a certain potter's art just as the modern trade-mark.

Beginning more than a half century ago in the old La Farge House in lower Broadway (where John La Farge was born) the house of Gilman Collamore and Company has done much to develop an appreciation of fine china in America. It was one of the first houses to bring over from England and France china, both modern and old, for its American clients. At this time many fine specimens of old china are on view as well as complete stocks from the modern English and Continental manufacture.

GILMAN COLLAMORE & COMPANY, Inc.
15 East 56th Street
New York

Germany and Austria

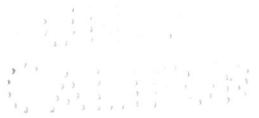

DRESDEN

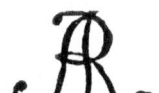

MEISSEN. Established in 1709. Mark used to 1712, in blue. Hard paste.

DRESDEN

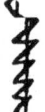

Mɛk used from 1712 to 1720, in blue. Hard paste.

DRESDEN

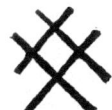

Abut 1720, mark in blue. Hard paste

DRESDEN

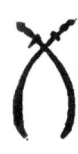

17ɔ, mark in blue. Hard paste.

DRESDEN

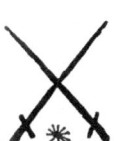

1796. MARCOLINI (Director) PERIOD. Mark in blue. Hard paste.

DRESDEN

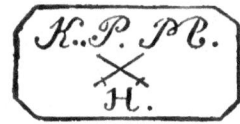

Royal pieces only. Mark in blue. Hard paste.

DRESDEN

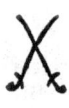

Present mark. This mark with two scratches across it shows imperfect pieces which may or may not have been decorated in the factory. Hard paste.

VIENNA

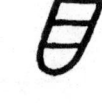

Established in 1718. This mark first used in 1744. Hard paste.

Royal factory discontinued in 1864.

BERLIN

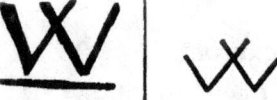

Established in 1751. Wegeleys' mark. Hard paste.

BERLIN

In 1763 became a royal establishment. Mark in blue. Sometimes an eagle added.

BERLIN

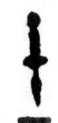

Different kind of sceptre. In blue. Hard paste.

BERLIN

An extra mark used in 1830 with the sceptre, which is the present mark. This mark complete is never used except with perfect pieces decorated in the factory. Decorated pieces bearing the blue sceptre mark only are decorated outside of the factory.

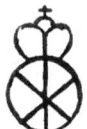

HOCHST, near MAYENCE

Founded in 1720. This mark, used about 1740, in gold, red, or blue. Hard paste.

HOCHST, near MAYENCE

Hard paste.

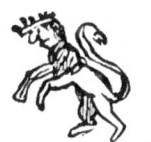

FRANKENTHAL

1755 to 1761. First period. Hard paste.

FRANKENTHAL

1799, second period. Carl Theodore. Hard paste.

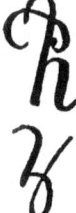

FRANKENTHAL

Phillipp Hanong (Director). Hard paste.

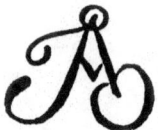

FRANKENTHAL

Joseph Adam Hanong (Director). Hard paste.

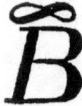

FRANKENTHAL

John Hanong (Director). Hard paste.

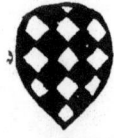

FRANKENTHAL

1800. Franz Bartolo (Director). Hard paste.

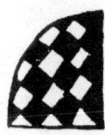

NYMPHENBURG

Established in 1747. Hard paste.

NYMPHENBURG

Hard paste.

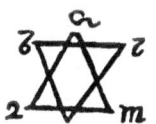

NYMPHENBURG

An early mark in blue. Hard paste.

FURSTENBURG

Established in 1750. Hard paste.

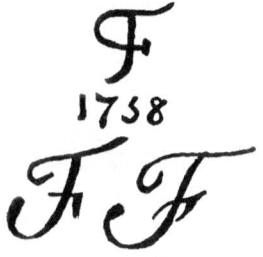

FURSTENBURG

1758. Hard paste.

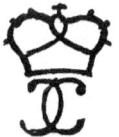

LUDWIGSBURG or KRONENBURG

Established in 1758 to 1806. Hard paste.

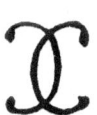 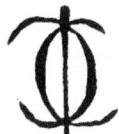

LUDWIGSBURG

First period. Hard paste.

LUDWIGSBURG

Second period.   Hard paste.

LUDWIGSBURG

Hard paste.   Mark in blue.

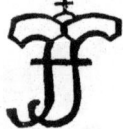

FULDA

Established in 1763 to 1780.   Hard paste.

FULDA

Hard paste.   The arms of Fulda.

RUDOLSTADT

Established in 1758.   Mark in blue. Hard paste.

RAUENSTEIN

Established in 1760.   Hard paste.

LIMBACH

Established   about   1761.   Hard paste.

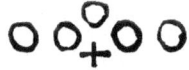

LIMBACH
Another mark. Hard paste.

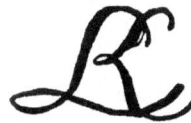

LIMBACH
Another mark. Hard paste.

GROSBREITENBACH
Established about 1770. Hard paste.

GROSBREITENBACH
Hard paste.

VOLKSTEDT
Established 1762. C. V. sometimes added with the arms. Hard paste.

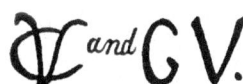

VOLKSTEDT
Another mark. Hard paste.

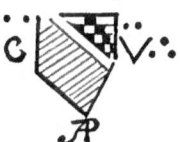

VOLKSTEDT
Another mark. Hard paste.

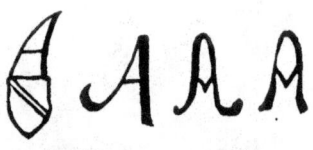

ANSPACH

Established about 1718. Hard paste.

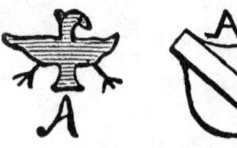

ANSPACH

Generally accompanied by letter A. Hard paste.

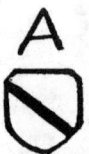

ANSPACH

Hard paste.

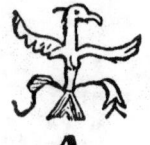

ANSPACH

Hard paste.

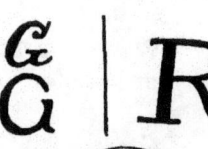

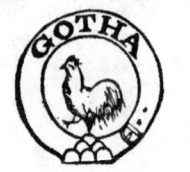

GOTHA

Founded in 1780. Hard paste. Various marks.

GERA

Established about 1780. Marks in blue. Hard paste.

ALT HALDENSTEBEN

The factory of M. Nathusins. Hard paste.

CHARLOTTENBURG

Established in 1790. Hard paste.

BADEN-BADEN

Established in 1753 to 1788. The edge of the ax in gold. Hard paste.

COLOGNE

Factory of M. L. Cremer. Enameled Fayence.

POPPLESDORF, near BONN

Fayence and porcelain.

STRASBOURG

Established about 1752. Hard paste.

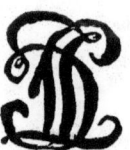

NIDERVILLER
Established in 1768.   Hard paste.

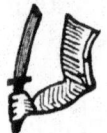

ELBOGEN in BOHEMIA
Established in 1815.   Hard paste.

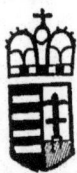

SCHLAKENWALD
Established about 1800.   Hard paste.

LEHAMMER
or PIRKENHAMMER, near CARLSBAD
Founded in 1802.   Hard paste.

HEREND
Established 1839.

HEREND
Another mark.

Russia and Poland

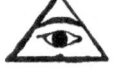

KORZEC

Established about 1803. Hard paste.

ПOSCOW

Established in 1787. Hard paste.

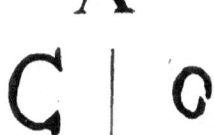

ST. PETERSBURG

Mark in blue. Hard paste.

ST. PETERSBURG

Mark of Empress Catherine II. 1762 to 1796. Mark in blue. Hard paste.

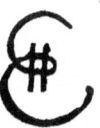

ST. PETERSBURG

Monogram of Nicholas I. 1825 to 1855.

ST. PETERSBURG

Established 1744. Mark in blue.

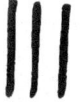

Denmark

COPENHAGEN

Established in 1772. Mark in blue. Hard paste.

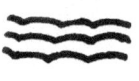

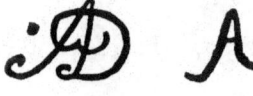

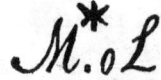

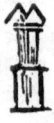

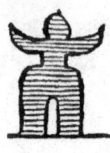

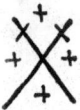

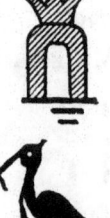

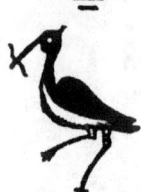

Holland and Belgium

AMSTERDAM

Established in 1782.   Mark in blue. Hard paste.

AMSTERDAM

Mark in blue.   Hard paste.

AMSTERDAM

Mark in blue.   Hard paste.

TOURNEY

Mark in gold represents a potter's kiln. Established in 1750. Soft paste.

TOURNEY

Mark in gold used after 1755.   Soft paste.

TOURNEY

Used about 1755.   Soft paste.

HAGUE

Factory established about 1775; ceased in 1785. Mark in gray. Hard paste.

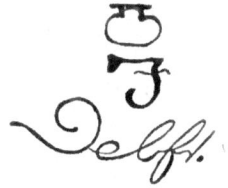

DELFT

Joost Thooft and Labouchere. Present mark Fayence.

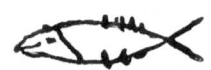

Switzerland

NYON

Established in 1790. Hard paste.

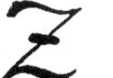

ZURICH

Established about 1759. Mark in blue. Hard paste.

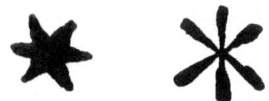

Italy and Spain

NOVE

1752. Mark in blue or red. Soft paste.

VENICE

Mark in red. Majolica.

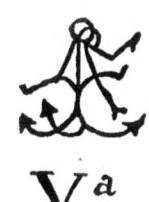

VENICE

Soft paste.

VENICE

1720 to 1740. Soft paste. Mark in red.

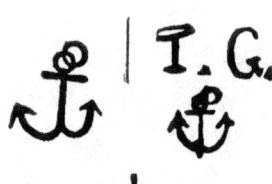

VENICE
Soft paste.   Mark in red.

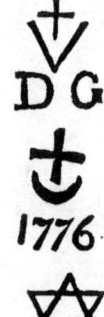

TURIN
Vineuf.   Established about 1770. Dr. Gioanetti (Director).   Soft paste.

TURIN
Vineuf. Another mark. Soft paste.

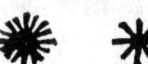

DOCCIA
Founded in 1735.   Hard and soft paste.

DOCCIA
Hard and soft paste.   Another mark.

GINORI.

DOCCIA
Hard and soft paste.   Another mark.

CAPO DI MONTE
Founded in 1736.   This mark used from 1759.   Factory abandoned in 1821.   Soft paste.

CAPO DI MONTE
Mark used from 1759.   Soft paste.

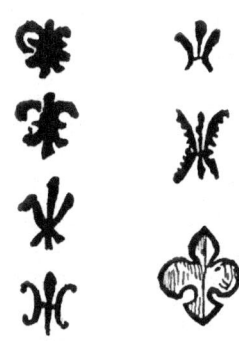

CAPO DI MONTE
Soft paste.   Other marks.

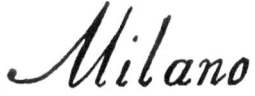

MILAN
Mark in blue.   Fayence.

MADRID
BUEN RETIRO.   Monogram of Charles III.   Established in 1759 to 1812.   Soft paste.

MADRID.

MADRID
Soft paste.   Another mark.

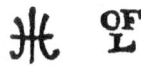

O. F L

MADRID
Mark in blue.   First quality. Soft paste.

MADRID
Mark in blue.   Soft paste.

MADRID

Mark in blue.   Mark under crown is another form of the monogram of Charles III., the founder.

OPORTO

Established about 1790. Hard paste. Mark in gold or colors.

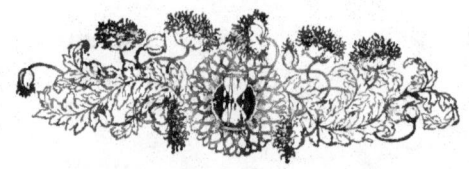

England

STAFFORDSHIRE

WEDGWOOD.

Established in 1769. This mark both stamped and printed.

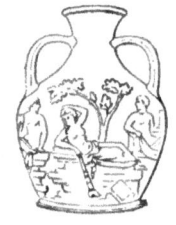

STAFFORDSHIRE

WEDGWOOD, present mark on decorated china.

TURNER.

STAFFORDSHIRE

Established about 1756.

W. ADAMS.

STAFFORDSHIRE

Established about 1780.

ROGERS.

STAFFORDSHIRE

Imitations of WEDGWOOD.

WOOD and CALDWELL.

STAFFORDSHIRE

Established in 1730.

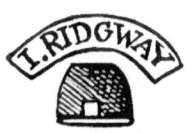

STAFFORDSHIRE

Established 1790.

LONGPORT.

STAFFORDSHIRE

Established in 1793 by Mr. John Davenport.

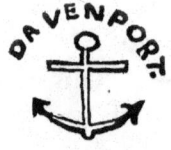

STAFFORDSHIRE

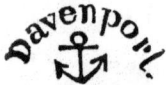

STAFFORDSHIRE

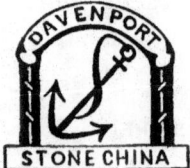

STAFFORDSHIRE

SPODE.

STAFFORDSHIRE

Established about 1770, by Josiah Spode.

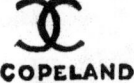

COPELAND

STAFFORDSHIRE

Copeland successor of Spode in 1833.

Richard ❤ Chaffers
17 69.

LIVERPOOL

Established in 1750.

SADLER
1756.

LIVERPOOL

Established in 1756.

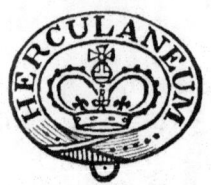

LIVERPOOL.

Established in 1790.

HERCULANEUM
POTTERY.

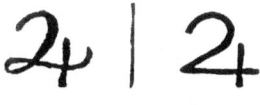

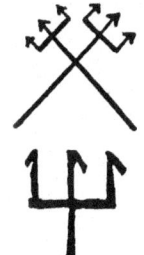

SWANSEA

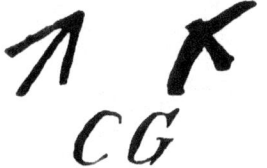

NANTGARW.

LIVERPOOL

This mark was used from 1822 to 1833.

PLYMOUTH

Established 1760. William Cookworthy.

YARMOUTH

Absolon, only a decorator.

SWANSEA

Established 1790. This mark used about 1815.

SWANSEA

Mark in red.

WALES

Established about 1813. Mark in red.

LEEDS

Hartley Greens & Co. Established about 1770.

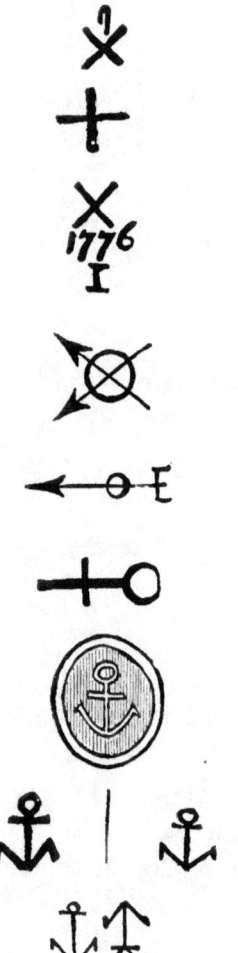

BRISTOL

Established about 1770, by Richard Champion.

BRISTOL

BRISTOL

Ceased in 1777.

BOW

Established about 1730. Ceased in 1775.

BOW

BOW

CHELSEA

The oldest mark.   About 1747.

CHELSEA

Mark in red.

CHELSEA

First quality mark in gold.

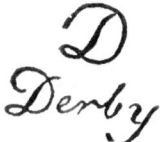

DERBY

Established 1751. This mark used before 1769.

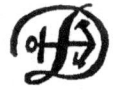

DERBY-CHELSEA

This mark in gold 1773.

CROWN DERBY

Mark in blue used about 1780.

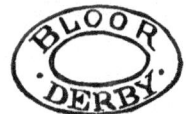

DERBY

Mark used in 1830. Bloor (Director).

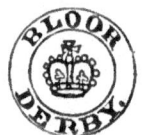

DERBY

Mark used in 1830. Bloor (Director).

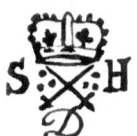

DERBY

Mark used in 1860.

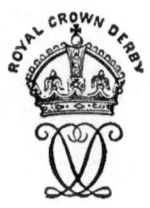

ROYAL CROWN DERBY

Present mark.

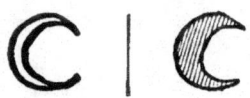

WORCESTER

Established 1751.   Oldest mark

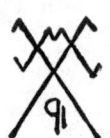

WORCESTER

Mark imitation of Dresden.

 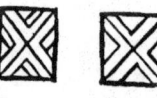

WORCESTER

Generally on Chinese patterns.

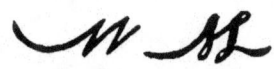

WORCESTER

About 1751.

C
Flight

WORCESTER

Used 1783 to 1788.

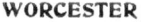

WORCESTER

Used 1807 to 1813.

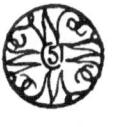 

WORCESTER

Used 1857 to 1862.

WORCESTER

Present mark.

CAUGHLEY. SHROPSHIRE

Established about 1751.

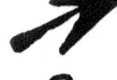

CAUGHLEY. SHROPSHIRE

An early mark in blue.

COALPORT

Established between 1780 and 1790.

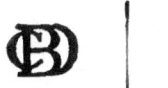

COALPORT

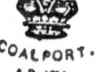

COALPORT

Present mark.

STAFFORDSHIRE

Established in 1791 by Mr. Thomas Minton.

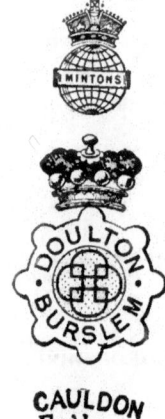

STAFFORDSHIRE

Present mark.

LAMBETH and BURSLEM

Doulton & Co.

STAFFORDSHIRE

Brown-Westhead, Moore & Co.

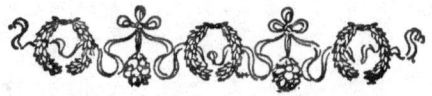

France

ST. CLOUD

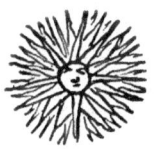

Established about 1695. Factory destroyed by fire in 1773; not rebuilt. Soft paste.

ST. CLOUD

S⁞C
T

This mark used from 1730 to 1762. Either in blue or graved in ware. The letter T stands for Tron, the name of the director. Soft paste.

CHANTILLY

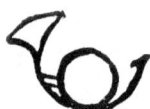

Established in 1735. Mark in blue or red. Soft paste.

ARRAS

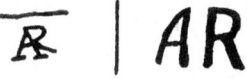

Established in 1782. Mark in blue. Factory ceased in 1786. Soft paste.

ΠENECY

D.V.

Established in 1735. This mark is usually impressed; sometimes traced in blue. Soft paste.

ETIOLLES, near CORBEIL

MP

Established in 1768. Monnier, manufacturer. Soft paste.

BR

OR

B la R

SX

⚓

SCEAUX.

BOURG LA REINE

Established in 1773. Jacques & Jullien. Soft paste.

SCEAUX-PENTHIEVRE, near PARIS

Established in 1750 by Jacques Capelle. These letters are engraved on the soft clay.

SCEAUX-PENTHIEVRE, near PARIS

The latter mark in blue. This mark occurs more frequently on Fayence.

CLINGNANCOURT

Established in 1775 by Pierre Deruelle. Mark in blue. Soft and hard paste.

CLINGNANCOURT

Used on pieces of Chinese style. Mark in red. Hard paste.

CLINGNANCOURT

Mark of Monsieur Comte de Provence.

ORLEANS

Established in 1753 by M. Gerré. Hard and soft paste.

ORLEANS

This mark used from 1808 to 1871, in blue or gold.

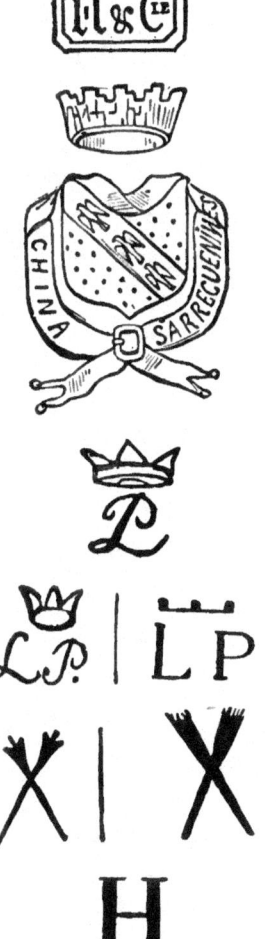

SARREGUEMINES

Soft paste.

SARREGUEMINES

Soft paste and Fayence.

VINCENNES

Soft paste.   Established in 1786.

VINCENNES

Soft paste.   Another mark.

PARIS. RUE FONTAINE AU ROY

Established in 1773 by Jean Baptiste Locré. Mark in blue. Hard paste.

PARIS. FAUBOURG ST. LAZARE

Founded in 1773.   Hard paste.

MAP

S

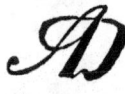

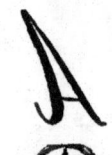

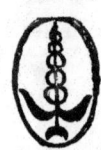

 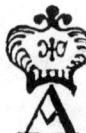

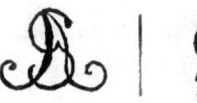

PARIS. FAUBOURG ST. ANTOINE

Established in 1773. Morelle, manufacturer. Hard paste.

PARIS. RUE DE LA ROQUETTE

Established in 1773. Souroux, manufacturer. Hard paste.

PARIS. GROS CAILLON

Established in 1773 by Advenir Lamarre. Hard paste.

PARIS. RUE DE CLICHY

Mark in blue. Hard paste.

FRANCE

A mark found on biscuit groups. Factory unknown.

PARIS. RUE THIROUX

Established in 1778. André Marie Lebeuf, manufacturer. Under the protection of Marie Antoinette. Mark in red. Hard paste.

PARIS. RUE DE BONDY

Established in 1780. Dihl and Guerhard, manufacturers. Under the patronage of Duc d'Angoulême. Hard paste.

PARIS. RUE DE BONDY

Another mark.   Hard paste.

PARIS. RUE DU FAUBOURG ST. DENIS

Established in 1769.   Under the protection of Charles Philippe Comte d'Artois, afterward Charles X.   Factory discontinued in 1810.

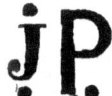

BELLEVILLE

Established in 1790 by Jacob Petit. Mark in blue.   Hard paste.

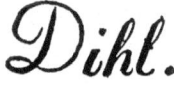

PARIS. RUE DE BONDY

Hard paste.   Mark in blue.

ROUEN

Under the reign of Louis XV.   Fayence.

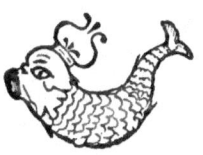

LILLE

Established in 1784 by Leperre Durot.   Mark in red.   Hard paste.

N...
à
Paris

PARIS

M. Nast, manufacturer. Mark in red. Hard paste.

halley

PARIS

Halley, manufacturer. First Empire mark in gold. Hard paste.

Em. Gallé

NANCY

Emile Gallé, manufacturer. Fayence and glass.

Sevres

Established at Vincennes in 1740.

Removed from there to Sevres in 1756.

King Louis XV. became sole proprietor in 1760.

Soft paste was made until 1805. Since then only hard paste.

The Sevres Marks

FIRST ROYAL EPOCH

1745 to 1792

VINCENNES.
The letter A denotes the year 1753,
continued to 1777. (Louis-XV.)

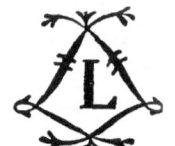

SEVRES.
Ornamented LL's.   Date 1764.

SEVRES. Date: 1778. (Louis XVI).
Double letters continued to 1793.

FIRST REPUBLICAN EPOCH

1792 to 1804

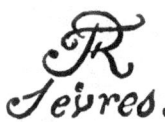

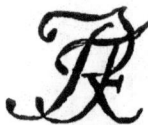

R.F
Sevres.

R.F
Sevres.

Sèvres

1792 to 1799.

MN^{1e}
Sèvres

1801 to 1804.

FIRST IMPERIAL EPOCH.
1804 TO 1814.

M.Imp^{le}
de Sevres.

NAPOLEON. 1804 to 1809.

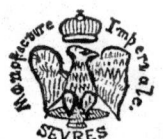

NAPOLEON. 1809 to 1814.

SECOND ROYAL EPOCH.
1814 TO 1848.

Louis XVIII 1814 to 1823.

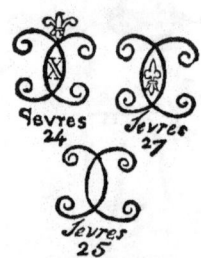

Charles X. 1824 to 1829.

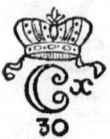

Charles X. 1829 and 1830.

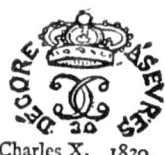

Charles X. 1830.

Louis Philippe. 1845-1848.

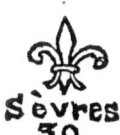

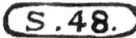

After 1848, this mark in green was
used for white porcelain.

Louis Philippe. 1831 to 1834.

SECOND REPUBLICAN EPOCH
1848 TO 1851.

The S stands for Sèvres, and 51 for
1851.

Louis Philippe. 1834-1835.

SECOND IMPERIAL EPOCH.
1852 TO 1872.

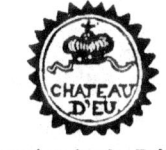

On services for the Palaces

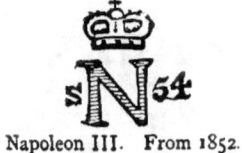

Napoleon III.   From 1852.

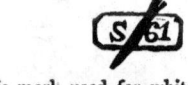

This mark used for white pieces;
when scratched it denotes issue
undecorated.

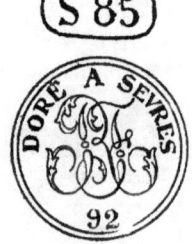

The marks
used at the
present time.

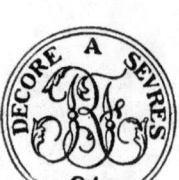

Unknown Marks

Chronological Table
Used in the Manufactory of Sevres

A (Vincennes) .	1753	P	.	.	. 1768	EE	. .	. 1782
B (ditto) .	1754	Q	.	.	. *1769	FF	. .	. 1783
C (ditto) .	1755	R	.	.	. 1770	GG	. .	. 1784
D . . .	1756	S	.	.	. 1771	HH	. .	. 1785
E . . .	1757	T	.	.	. 1772	II	. .	. 1786
F . . .	1758	U	.	.	. 1773	JJ	. .	. 1787
G . . .	1759	V	.	.	. 1774	KK	. .	. 1788
H . . .	1760	X	.	.	. 1775	LL	. .	. 1789
I . . .	1761	Y	.	.	. 1776	MM	. .	. 1790
J . . .	1762	Z	.	.	. 1777	NN	. .	. 1791
K . . .	1763	AA	.	.	. 1778	OO	. .	. 1792
L . . .	1764	BB	.	.	. 1779	PP	. .	. 1793
M . . .	1765	CC	.	.	. 1780	QQ	. .	. 1794
N . . .	1766	DD	.	.	. 1781	RR	. .	. 1795
O . . ,	1767							

Year IX ...1801... T 9		1807 7
		1808 . . . ⸤ . 8
" X ...1802... X		1809 9
		1810 10
" XI ...1803... 11		1811 . (onze) . . o.z.
		1812 . (douze) . . d.z.
" XII ...1804... -//-		1813 . (treize) . . t z.
		1814 . (quatorze) . . q.z.
" XIII ...1805... ↑		1815 . (quinze) . . q.n.
		1816 . (seize) . . s.z.
" XIV ...1806... ⚌		1817 . (dix sept) . . d.s.

From this date the year is expressed by the last two figures only,—thus, 18 for 1818, etc.,—up to the present time.

---

* This comet was sometimes substituted for the ordinary mark of the letter Q.